6748
Wild Bill Hickok

Carl R. Green
AR B.L.: 4.5
Points: 1.0

OUTLAWS AND LAWMEN
· OF THE WILD WEST ·

WILD BILL HICKOK

REVISED EDITION

By Carl R. Green and William R. Sanford

Enslow Publishers, Inc.
40 Industrial Road
Box 398
Berkeley Heights, NJ 07922
USA

http://www.enslow.com

Original edition published in 1992.

Library of Congress Cataloging-in-Publication Data
Green, Carl R.
  Wild Bill Hickok / Carl R. Green and William R. Sanford. — Rev. ed.
    p. cm. — (Outlaws and lawmen of the wild West)
  Summary: "Readers will find out about the life of Wild Bill Hickok, a scout, lawman, and showman of the Wild West"—Provided by publisher.
  Includes bibliographical references and index.
  ISBN 978-0-7660-3177-7
  1. Hickok, Wild Bill, 1837–1876—Juvenile literature. 2. Peace officers—West (U.S.)—Biography—Juvenile literature. 3. Frontier and pioneer life—West (U.S.)—Juvenile literature. 4. West (U.S.)—Biography—Juvenile literature. 5. West (U.S.)—History—1860–1890—Juvenile literature. I. Sanford, William R. (William Reynolds), 1927– II. Title.
  F594.H62G743 2009
  978'.02092—dc22
  [B]
                        2008010009

ISBN-10: 0-7660-3177-2

Printed in the United States of America

10 9 8 7 6 5 4 3 2 1

To Our Readers:
We have done our best to make sure all Internet Addresses in this book were active and appropriate when we went to press. However, the authors and the publisher have no control over and assume no liability for the material available on those Internet sites or on other Web sites they may link to. Any comments or suggestions can be sent by e-mail to comments@enslow.com or to the address on the back cover.

♻ Enslow Publishers, Inc., is committed to printing our books on recycled paper. The paper in every book contains 10% to 30% post-consumer waste (PCW). The cover board on the outside of each book contains 100% PCW. Our goal is to do our part to help young people and the environment too!

Interior photos: Alamy/William S. Kuta, p. 10; Alamy/Niday Picture Library, p. 17; Alamy/North Wind Picture Archives, p. 33; Alamy/Don Smetzer, p. 44; The Bridgeman Art Library International/Private Collection, Peter Newark American Pictures, p. 36; The Granger Collection, New York, p. 25; iStockphoto/spxChrome, (marshal badge), odd pages; iStockphoto/Alex Bramwell (revolver), even pages; iStockphoto/billnoll (frame), pp. 4, 11, 23; Legends of America, pp. 1, 5, 6, 7, 11, 15, 16, 23, 30, 31, 35, 38, 40, 41; Library of Congress, p. 27; North Wind Picture Archives/NorthWind, pp. 9, 13, 19, 20; Shutterstock/Dhoxax (background), pp. 3, 5, 8–9, 16–17, 23, 29, 36–37, 43.

Cover photo: Legends of America (*James Butler "Wild Bill" Hickok had his picture taken many times, more than most other figures of his day. As a lawman, he liked to dress in fine clothes.*)

TABLE OF CONTENTS

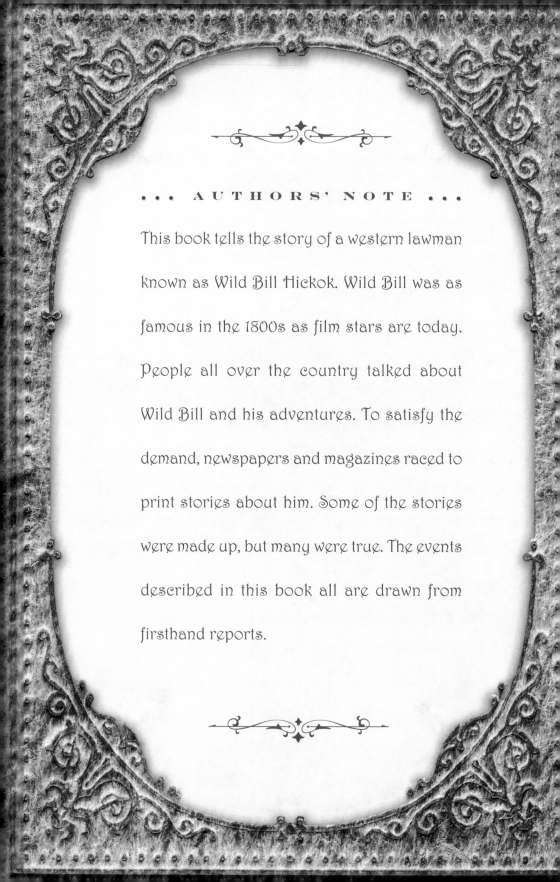

. . . A U T H O R S ' N O T E . . .

This book tells the story of a western lawman

known as Wild Bill Hickok. Wild Bill was as

famous in the 1800s as film stars are today.

People all over the country talked about

Wild Bill and his adventures. To satisfy the

demand, newspapers and magazines raced to

print stories about him. Some of the stories

were made up, but many were true. The events

described in this book all are drawn from

firsthand reports.

CHAPTER ONE

YOUNG HICKOK HITS THE BULLSEYE

James Butler Hickok was eighteen years old in the spring of 1855. Having just left home, he took a job tending cattle in Kansas. When asked his name, he answered, "Bill Hickok."

The people of Kansas were about to vote for or against slavery. Bill had grown up hating the South's practice of keeping slaves. He wanted Kansas to be a free state.

While still a young man, James Butler Hickok proved that he was a skilled marksman. He was in his early twenties when he posed for this portrait.

In the 1850s, Border Ruffians from Missouri (above) tried to turn Kansas into a slave state. Young Bill Hickok volunteered to join the fight against the Ruffians.

Making things even more complicated, armed men from Missouri were crossing the border to promote slavery. To fight these Border Ruffians, Colonel James Lane was recruiting a Free State Army.

Bill tried to join Lane's army. An officer smiled and told him the army did not take kids. He also said that Lane's men had to furnish their own horses. This was bad news, because Bill did not own a horse. In fact, he had only $32 in his pocket. It was a month's pay, but it was not enough to buy a horse.

Lane's recruits were holding a shooting match on the edge of town. Bill walked out to watch. When he saw how bad the shooting was, he paid $30 to enter the contest. Paying the entry fee left him with only $2, but he had faith in his skill with a rifle.

When Bill's turn came, he hit the bullseye with his first shot. No one else could match him. In the last event, the target was a rolling piece of wood. Again, Bill's shot hit the mark. The soldiers gathered around and cheered. They said that Colonel Lane needed men who could shoot straight. Bill told them that he wanted to join, but he did not have a horse. "Yes, you do!" someone yelled. That was when Bill learned that he had won first prize—a fine bay horse.

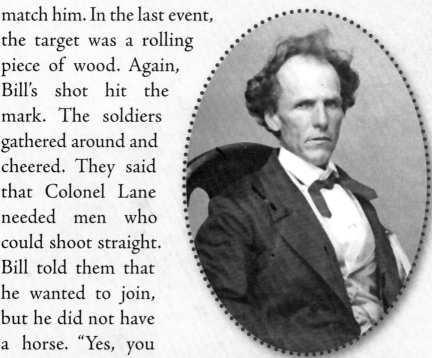

Once Colonel James Lane (above) found out how good Bill was with a gun, he let him join his Free State Army.

Young Bill Hickok became one of Colonel Lane's most trusted soldiers. When the colonel spoke in public, it was Bill who stood guard. The eighteen-year-old was fast making a name for himself as a gunslinger.

WILD BILL GROWS UP

Wild Bill Hickok was born in Illinois on May 27, 1837. William and Polly Hickok named their fifth son James Butler Hickok.

William and Polly had come to Illinois from Vermont. As a young man, William had studied to be a preacher. He had to change his plans when typhoid fever left him in poor health. He moved his wife and four boys to Homer, Illinois, in 1836. James was born there a year later. Over the next few years, Polly also gave birth to two girls, for a total of seven children. On today's maps, Homer is known as Troy Grove.

William ran a country store, but he lost the store in 1837. Those were hard times, and William turned to farming to make a living. Because his health was poor, his sons had to help work the fields. Farm work came before schooling, but Polly made sure that James learned to read and write.

The Hickoks did what they could to fight slavery. William turned the farm into a stop on the Underground

There were many "stations" on the Underground Railroad in the northern states. The Hickoks' farm in Illinois was one of them.

Railroad. Runaway slaves hid in the cellar on their way north to freedom in Canada. Young James helped guide the runaways to their next hiding place.

By the time he was twelve, James was a crack shot. When he went hunting the Hickoks could count on eating well. James also made good money with his rifle and Colt pistol. In those days the government paid hunters fifty cents for each wolf they killed. Because wounded wolves sometimes attacked their hunters, James learned to make every shot count.

James worked as a mule driver for a company that was digging a canal. It may have looked like this old canal in Maryland.

William Hickok died when James was fourteen. By then James's brother Oliver had left to join the California Gold Rush. His brothers Horace and Lorenzo helped when they could, but they had their own farms to work. James put meat on the family table by hunting deer and rabbits. Unable to keep the farm going, Polly moved the few miles back to Homer. James missed the freedom he had known on the farm. He thought town life was boring.

In 1855, James found work as a mule driver. The company that hired him was digging a canal. Before long, the boy found himself being bullied by an older driver. One of Charles Hudson's "jokes" was to push James into the canal. When Hudson tried this a second time, James fought back. During the wrestling match that followed, both men fell into the canal. The other workers quickly pulled James out of the water. By the time they reached Hudson, he seemed to have stopped breathing.

Fearful that he had killed the bully, James ran home. After packing his clothes and guns, he wrote a note to his mother and left town. If he had returned to the canal he might have torn up the note. Hudson, it turned out, was still alive.

James walked all the way to the

At 21, Bill Hickok was a tall, handsome young man. He learned the lawman's trade by serving as town constable in Monticello, Kansas.

city of St. Louis, Missouri. Then he moved on to Kansas. There he joined Jim Lane's army and helped make Kansas a free state. For his own reasons, James stuck with the story that his first name was Bill. Perhaps he used the name in honor of his father. On legal papers, though, he signed his name, "J. B. Hickok."

By 1858, Bill Hickok had grown to just over six feet. His body was strong and athletic. He had cold blue eyes and long, golden-brown hair. A mustache hid his full upper lip. Women admired his good looks—and his cleanliness. Most men bathed just once a week, but Bill took a daily bath whenever he could.

After he left the Free State Army, Bill claimed some land near Monticello, Kansas. He earned his living by helping the local farmers. While serving as town constable, he also made enemies. Twice someone burned his cabin while he was away.

Bill Hickok did not rebuild the cabin a third time. Instead, he set about learning to drive a stagecoach. He soon became an expert with the reins and long whip drivers used to control their teams. Bill's first run ended at the fifty-mile mark. At that point a second driver took his place. When the return stage arrived, he drove it back to his home base.

The stage run was dull, hard work. When he was given the chance to drive a freight wagon to Santa Fe, New Mexico, Bill jumped at it. The run covered 680 adventurous miles. The freight wagons carried goods for

As a freight driver on the Santa Fe Trail in 1859–1860, Bill had his fair share of adventures. The trail was a major route for transporting goods, as well as settlers (above).

both traders and settlers. At night, the drivers drew the wagons into a circle. The horses and oxen grazed safely inside the ring of wagons.

One day Bill saw a driver hit a young boy. Bill was fond of children and he hated bullies. He slugged the man and knocked him down. The boy thanked Bill and introduced himself as William Cody. Young Cody went on to become the famous scout and showman, Buffalo Bill.

On another trip, Bill heard a sound like thunder. He turned and saw that Indians had stampeded a herd of buffalo. The huge herd was sweeping down on the wagon train. Bill set his brake and held the oxen still. As he had hoped, the herd parted as it reached the wagons. Bill then picked up his rifle and shot a big bull. That night he dined on buffalo steak for the first time.

On a trip to Santa Fe, Bill met one of his heroes. He was Kit Carson, the famous mountain man and explorer. The two men took in the town's sights and relaxed at a local dance hall. Carson warned his new friend that many good men had died in the town's drunken brawls. Rather than take a chance, Bill left before the nightly fights broke out.

Bill next took on the risky job of driving a stage through the Rocky Mountains. On one trip, his stagecoach began slipping on ice at Raton Pass. To make matters worse, a runaway freight wagon was sliding down the hill toward him. Bill urged his mules into a trot. Somehow he kept the stage from flying off the narrow, icy trail. As he rounded a bend, the runaway wagon flew off the cliff.

The Raton Pass was always hazardous. On a fall day in 1860, Bill's horse threw him when it was spooked by a female grizzly. The bear, who was protecting her cub, caught Bill before he could run. He fired his pistol into the bear's huge body and slashed her with his knife. Maddened by the pain, the grizzly raked him with her sharp claws. With hope dying, Hickok plunged his knife deep into the crazed bear's stomach.

A wagon driver found Bill pinned beneath the dead bear. His scalp was torn and his left arm was crushed. The driver lifted him into the wagon

Kit Carson was a famous mountain man and explorer. He also was one of Bill's heroes.

and drove him to Santa Fe. Doctors said he was a goner, but Bill Hickok refused to die. Sent back to Kansas City, he soon regained his health.

CHAPTER THREE

THE CIVIL WAR YEARS

The Civil War began in April 1861. Bill Hickok wanted to join the fight against slavery, but he was still laid up with his wounds. While his arm healed, he worked at Rock Creek, Nebraska. That was the summer he killed Dave McCanles in a famous shoot-out. McCanles made the mistake of trying to bully Hickok. He also made threats against Horace Wellman, one of Bill's friends.

During the Civil War, Bill took up the risky job of scouting for the Union Army.

When Bill joined the army in the fall of 1861, the war was going badly for the North. In July the Union Army had suffered a major defeat at the Battle of Bull Run in Manassas, Virginia (above).

The trouble came to a head on July 12. When McCanles barged into Wellman's house, Bill told the bully to leave. McCanles refused. Bill shrugged and stepped behind a curtain. Puzzled by the move, McCanles did not know what to do. When he did step forward, his hand was moving toward his gun. Bill fired through the curtain, hitting the big man in the chest. A jury agreed that he fired in self-defense.

The Civil War was going badly for the North in the fall of 1861. Bill joined the Union Army and was put to work leading army wagon trains. One trip took him to Independence, Missouri. While he was there, he saw a mob on its way to hang a friend of his. The friend was a bartender who had wounded a gunman in a barroom brawl. Bill drew his pistol and aimed it at the mob's leaders. The ruffians could see that he meant business. They turned and went off to find their fun elsewhere.

The town was soon buzzing with the news of Bill's brave stand. When he rode out of town, people cheered. A woman yelled, "Good for you, Wild Bill!" From that time on, that is what most people called him.

Craving more excitement, Wild Bill Hickok became an army scout. His task was to find out what enemy units were doing. That meant riding far behind rebel lines in southwest Missouri and Arkansas. For Wild Bill, it was a time of close calls and great adventures. As the stories were told and retold, they became the stuff of legend.

On one trip, Wild Bill heard that a rebel captain was carrying secret papers. With the help of two other scouts, he set up an ambush. As the captain and his soldiers rode past, the scouts yelled and fired their pistols. The surprised rebels fled. Bill gave chase and caught the captain. Knife in hand, he slit the man's coat open and took the papers.

Now Wild Bill had to find his way back to the Union lines. As he rode northward, he spotted four rebel soldiers outside a farm cabin. Two girls were cooking for them. Bill took the rebels captive, tied them up, and ate their lunch. He also flirted with the girls—and almost stayed too long. A second group of rebels rode up and opened fire. One of their bullets killed Bill's horse. He escaped when one of the girls gave him her horse.

Bill liked to tell stories about his adventures while scouting for the Union Army. It was dangerous work, and Bill was good at it. This illustration shows a typical army scout in the West in the late 1800s–early 1900s.

Wild Bill sometimes dressed in a rebel uniform. In Arkansas one summer, he was arrested as a spy. A military court ordered him put to death. On the night before he was to die, Bill managed to cut the ropes that bound him. Then he killed a guard and changed into the man's clothes. When the firing squad arrived the next morning, Bill was gone.

Gunfights like the one shown above were a common occurrence in the lawless towns on the frontier. Wild Bill found himself involved in one with a former friend in July 1865.

In late 1863, Wild Bill was carrying dispatches in an area controlled by Union troops. To his surprise he ran into a Confederate raiding party. Before the rebels could react, Bill shot two of them. The third man spurred his horse and tried to escape, but Bill knew a shortcut. When the two men met, both opened fire. The rebel missed, but Bill did not. When he left he was riding the dead man's horse. The mare was tough, fast, and easy to train. Bill named her Black Nell.

For his next mission, Wild Bill returned to Arkansas. He called himself Amos Jones and joined the rebel army. Wearing Confederate grey allowed him to spy on the enemy's movements. In the spring of 1864, he was wounded while returning to Union lines. After his wound healed, the army sent him off on more scouting trips.

The long, bitter war ended in April 1865. Wild Bill was living in Springfield, Missouri. With nowhere else to call home, he stayed there. Springfield was a rough town. Many of the men who lived there had been soldiers. Most carried guns.

One of Wild Bill's friends was a gambler named Dave Tutt. Bill borrowed money from Tutt and bought a saddle from him on credit. Then, almost without warning, Tutt turned against his friend. Some people said it was because both men were courting Susanna Moore. Quite likely, Susanna was the girl who had given her horse to Bill during the war.

Both men liked to play poker. Because of Tutt's bad temper, Wild Bill refused to play with him. That made Tutt even angrier. When Bill sat in on a game, Tutt would tell the other men how to play their hands. He was clearly trying to start a fight.

Susanna warned Wild Bill that Tutt planned to kill him in a gunfight. If it was a fair fight he would not go to jail. Bill assured her that he would not start a fight. Susanna believed him. She knew he would not run from one, either.

One night, Tutt loaned $200 to one of Wild Bill's opponents. The cards ran against the man and Bill won all of the money. That was too much for Tutt. He demanded that Bill pay him the $40 he owed for the saddle. Bill calmly handed him the money. Then Tutt said he wanted the $35 Bill also owed him. Bill told him it was only $25—and that he had a paper to prove it. Tutt picked up Bill's watch from the table. He said he would hold it until Bill came back with the paper. Tutt was gone when Bill returned. So was the watch.

The two men came face-to-face in the town square on July 21, 1865. Wild Bill could see that the gambler was ready to fight. Tutt was holding Bill's watch in one hand and a pistol in the other. At a range of seventy-five yards, Tutt pulled the trigger. The shot missed. Cool as always, Bill took careful aim. His bullet smashed into the gambler's heart.

As the crowd watched, Wild Bill picked up his watch. Then he turned himself in to the sheriff. At the trial, the jury decided that Bill had fired in self-defense. Free once more, he stayed in town for the rest of the year. Then he mounted Black Nell and headed toward Fort Riley, Kansas.

CHAPTER FOUR

LAWMAN AND INDIAN SCOUT

ild Bill Hickok arrived at Fort Riley during the winter of 1866. The post was in turmoil. Soldiers bored with peacetime army life were deserting. Some of them took army horses and mules with them when they left.

Captain Richard Owen welcomed his old friend. He asked Wild Bill to serve as a deputy U.S. marshal. As a law officer, Bill was in charge of restoring order at the fort. One big challenge was that of catching deserters

Wherever Wild Bill went, people turned to him for protection and trusted him to restore order.

and horse thieves. The salary for this dangerous work was only $75 a month.

Wild Bill pinned on his lawman's star. Then he went after the latest mule thieves. He caught up with them two days later. When they saw who was chasing them, they gave up without a fight. Bill took the thieves and the stolen mules back to Fort Riley.

With Wild Bill on duty, desertions and thefts slowed down. In his spare time, he guided tourists across the plains. Dr. William Finlaw, the post doctor, also used Bill's services. Bill guarded Finlaw and his family when the doctor moved between forts. At night, he slept under Finlaw's wagon to protect the children.

Early in the new year, Wild Bill tracked two hundred stolen horses and mules to a distant valley. With the help of army scouts, he recovered the entire herd. He later said that the outlaws had been ready to fight for the valuable animals. That did not bother Bill and the scouts. Their accurate rifle fire drove the thieves away.

Each week seemed to bring a new adventure. One winter day, Wild Bill spotted a runaway stagecoach. Urging Black Nell into a gallop, he caught the speeding stage. As Nell kept pace, Bill swung himself up to the driver's seat. Then he grabbed the reins and brought the panicky horses to a stop. The frightened driver showed Bill that his hands were frozen. With Nell trotting behind the stage, Bill drove the man to a doctor.

In 1868, Wild Bill agreed to umpire a baseball game. In those days many games ended in riots, but Bill kept the players under control. The game pictured here was played in New Jersey in 1866.

On a Saturday in 1868, Wild Bill umpired a baseball game in Kansas City. The game matched the home team against a team from Atchison, Kansas. In those days, baseball games often turned into riots. No one, however, dared to argue with this umpire's calls. Kansas City won the high-scoring game, 48 to 28. As payment, Bill was driven back to town in a carriage pulled by a team of white horses.

This was the era of railroad building in the West. The first train had steamed into Fort Riley just before

Wild Bill arrived. Now, as the steel rails moved westward, the Plains Indians were fighting to save their land.

General Winfield Scott Hancock was charged with bringing peace to the plains. Wild Bill was not impressed. He thought Hancock looked more at home behind a desk than on a horse.

Hancock picked the headstrong George Armstrong Custer to lead the 7th Cavalry. Wild Bill signed on as General Custer's scout. He rode out ahead of the troops, looking for Indian campsites and trails. After each foray he reported his findings to the general.

When Custer sent messages to Fort Riley, it was Wild Bill's job to carry them. He rode by night and hid by day, but the tactic sometimes failed. Once a raiding party of six warriors rode into the valley where Bill was hiding. Bill drew his pistols and fired, killing two of them. The others fled, but the shots attracted more warriors. Only Nell's speed saved Bill's scalp that day.

On another trip, Wild Bill was out on the plains when he heard the sound of stampeding buffalo. Nell carried him clear of the herd—and into the path of three Indians. More braves soon joined the chase. This time, Bill saw that Nell could not outrun them. He jumped down and told the horse to lie on her side. When the Indians closed in, he opened fire. With three braves dead, the survivors rode away.

The Indian wars dragged on. Despite its best efforts, the army could not subdue the Plains tribes. General

Hancock blamed Custer for the failure. He court-martialed General Custer and removed him from his command.

Hancock was replaced in 1867 by General Philip Sheridan. The new general hoped to sign a peace treaty with the tribal chiefs who had gathered for talks. To keep the peace, the federal government sent gifts of food and ammunition to the

General George Custer (left) was a friend of Wild Bill, but Tom Custer (standing) did not respect the lawman's authority. The Custer brothers are pictured with the general's wife, Libbie.

tribes. Wild Bill said that only madmen would give bullets to the Indians. True to his warning, the tribes soon returned to the warpath.

Sheridan recalled General Custer to duty in 1868. He needed fighters and Custer was fearless. Wild Bill was still carrying messages, but the work bored him. He was pleased to learn that Sheridan was about to march against the tribes. He wanted to be a scout again.

Wild Bill kept busy while he waited for the campaign to begin. He was leading a group of settlers one day when the Cheyenne attacked. After he and the settlers drove the Indians back with rifle fire, Bill pursued the retreating raiders. All at once, three braves turned back and closed in on him. An arrow hit Bill in the thigh and he fell off his horse. The Indians thought he was dead. When they moved in to scalp him, Bill gunned down all three. That night Bill rode through the Indian lines to bring help to the settlers.

The wound did not keep Wild Bill out of the saddle for long. On a trip out of Fort Lyon in 1869, he took a chance on riding by day. It was March, and he knew the Indian ponies were in poor shape after a hard winter. At least one band of Cheyenne was far from their winter camp, however. The braves saw his campfire and crept up on him. In a hand-to-hand fight, Bill shot three Cheyenne. The next thing he knew, the war chief was plunging a spear into his hip. Despite the pain, Bill kept on shooting. He later claimed that he had killed all seven of his attackers.

Wild Bill pulled himself into the saddle and rode to Fort Lyon. A doctor shook his head as he cleaned the deep wound. Bill's scouting days were over for a while.

CHAPTER FIVE

LAWLESS TOWNS NEED STRONG SHERIFFS

Hays City, Kansas, was founded in 1867. The town was one of the jumping-off points for the Santa Fe Trail. Its warehouses stored goods waiting to be shipped westward.

The town was a violent place, even by the standards of the Old West. Hays City had no sheriff and no courts. The two main streets were lined with saloons and dance halls. Gamblers and dance-hall girls preyed on patrons with money in their pockets. Drunken cowboys celebrated their night on the town by firing pistols into the air. Murder and theft were daily events.

The locals knew something had to be done. They sent the town's leaders to talk to Wild Bill. Would he help them clean up the place? Perhaps Wild Bill was tired of Indian fighting. He took the job as acting sheriff of Ellis County in 1869.

When he lived in town, Wild Bill dressed like a gentleman. He traded his buckskins for a black coat and

In 1869, Wild Bill moved to Hays City, Kansas (above). It was a tough, lawless town—and clearly in need of a fearless lawman.

a wide-brimmed hat. A proud man, he wore handmade boots that showed off his small feet. A red sash at his waist held two pearl-handled Colt pistols. To top off his outfit, Bill often added a silk-lined cape.

With Wild Bill on the job, Hays City settled down. The town still had its share of hard, tough men, however. Saloon owner Bill Curry was one of them. One day Bill told Curry to fire the crooked dealers who worked for him. Curry did not take kindly to the order. The next time Wild Bill played cards in his saloon, Curry pointed a pistol at the sheriff's head. All the card players froze, but Bill turned the threat into

As acting sheriff of Ellis County, Kansas, Wild Bill dressed the part. He traded in his buckskins for a gentleman's outfit.

a joke. He laughed and offered to buy drinks for everyone. Curry shook Bill's hand and called off the feud.

Wild Bill's run-in with Jack Strawhun did not end quite as well. Strawhun often bragged about the men he had killed. One time when Strawhun was fighting drunk, Bill helped tie him to a post. Afterward, Strawhun swore to kill the sheriff.

The next time they met in a saloon Strawhun raised his pistol. With his life on the line, Bill fired first. That night the town band put on a concert in his honor.

The troops from Fort Hays also caused trouble. General Custer's brother Tom was the biggest offender. Tom felt sure that the general's fame would protect him. In July 1870, Tom rode his horse into a billiard parlor. When the horse balked at jumping over a table, he shot it. Wild Bill hauled the young man before a judge. Tom paid his fine, but swore he would get even.

A few nights later, Tom's soldier friends jumped Wild Bill as he entered a saloon. Bill shook them off and shot two before the rest fled. After their narrow escape, the soldiers vowed vengeance. Bill's friends warned him that he could not fight the entire U.S. Army. Wild Bill agreed that a dead sheriff would not be of much use. He packed his gear and caught a train out of town.

Abilene, Kansas, at the end of the Chisholm Trail, was the first great cowtown. Texas cowboys drove their herds of longhorn cattle north and sold them in Abilene. Then they bathed, put on fancy clothes, and buckled on their guns. They would have felt undressed without them. With money in their pockets, the cowboys played cards, danced, and drank lots of cheap whiskey. When they tired of firing at the sky, they were likely to shoot at each other.

In 1870, Tom Smith became Abilene's first marshal. He was murdered six months later. The next two marshals came and went even more quickly. In April 1871, the mayor sent for Wild Bill. Bill looked the town over and said he would take the job. Abilene paid him $150 a month and 25 percent of

Abilene, Kansas, was a "cowtown." Cowboys from Texas drove their herds to Abilene to be shipped by railroad (above) to eastern markets.

the fines he collected. The salary more than doubled his Hays City wages.

In April, Abilene was a quiet town of 500 people. Wild Bill had time to learn his way around. The railroad tracks cut the town in half. To the south were the saloons, gambling halls, and boardinghouses. Homes, shops, and churches lay to the north.

The peace was shattered when the first herds arrived in May. By June, 7,000 newcomers had crowded into town. Wild Bill and his three deputies were busy night and day. It helped that only lawmen were allowed to carry guns. Even so, enforcing gun laws in a town full of cowboys was far from easy.

One gunslinger who ignored the law was John Wesley Hardin. Young Hardin was said to have killed seven men on his way north from Texas. Ben Thompson, a saloon owner, tried to talk Hardin into killing Wild Bill. Hardin refused, saying he had no quarrel with the marshal. He did insist on wearing his guns. When Bill saw the Texan, he ordered him to hand over his guns. Hardin, who was no fool, decided not to risk a shoot-out. He gave up his guns without a fight.

Wild Bill did his best to keep the gambling halls honest. He watched the games closely and cracked down on cheating. This cost the owners money, and they vowed to get even. Bill guessed they would pay a gunman to kill him. To avoid an ambush, he always walked in the center of the street. He also carried a shotgun and stayed clear of open doorways. When he played cards, he sat with his back to the wall. Careless lawmen often died young.

Abilene always threw itself a party at the end of the year's cattle drives. Wild Bill set down only one rule: no shooting. The whiskey flowed and the crowd seemed to be having a noisy good time. Then Bill heard shooting outside the Alamo Saloon. He found Ben

Thompson's partner, Phil Coe, with a gun in his hand. When Coe took a shot at him, Bill returned the fire. Coe fell with two bullets in his stomach.

A second man rushed toward Wild Bill from the darkness. Wild Bill fired again. A moment later, he saw that he had killed Special Deputy Mike Williams. Mike was one of Bill's best friends.

The pointless death saddened Wild Bill. He could not forgive himself for shooting a friend. That same night he turned in his badge. His career as a lawman was over.

John Wesley Hardin was a well-known Texas gunslinger. In Abilene he chose not to test Wild Bill's marksmanship.

CHAPTER SIX

A SHOWMAN COMES TO THE END OF THE TRAIL

In the 1870s, Wild West shows that featured cowboys and Indians were all the rage. Shows that starred well-known western heroes drew the biggest crowds. Wild Bill Hickok was one of these big names. He was often featured in the magazines and dime novels of the day. When writers dropped by, Wild Bill told them tall tales about his adventures. Quite often the stories grew taller and wilder in the telling.

This dime novel was published twenty years after Wild Bill's death in 1876. Even during his lifetime, people loved to read about his adventures.

"Diamond Dick, Jr.'s Mysterious Diagram," in No. 191 of this Library.

DIAMOND-DICK
LIBRARY

No. 192.   Street & Smith, Publishers.   NEW YORK.   25 Vesey St., N. Y.   5 Cents.

Wild Bill's Last Trail.

By NED BUNTLINE.

In 1872, Colonel Sidney Barnett hired Wild Bill to put on a Wild West show. The show was booked for New York's Niagara Falls. The local hotel owners wanted to attract more tourists to the falls. A Wild West show sounded like a surefire hit.

Wild Bill said he would put on a buffalo roundup. Out on the plains, he found that shooting buffalo was easy compared to lassoing them. Once, when Bill roped a buffalo, it flipped his horse head over heels. In time, Bill and his men learned to lasso buffalo by the horns. Then they loaded the big animals into boxcars and shipped them to New York. To Bill's dismay, many died on the way.

The show ran for two days in August. Wild Bill put on a fringed buckskin suit and announced the events. Cowboys chased and roped wild Texas steers. Then the buffalo were turned loose. Indians wearing war paint mounted their mustangs and chased the herd. As they closed in they shot blunt arrows at the buffalo. When the animals tired, the Indians roped them.

All agreed that it was a fine show. The crowd clapped for war dances, a lacrosse game, and music played by a brass band. For real drama, a dancing bear broke loose and chased a sausage seller. In the end, the show failed because very few tickets were sold. Most of the crowd watched for free from behind a fence. Bill sold the buffalo and returned to the plains.

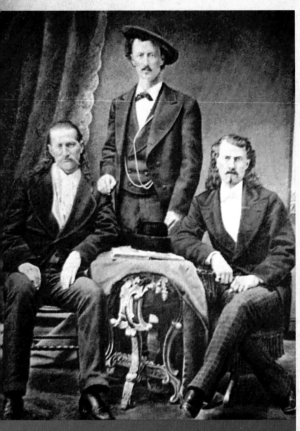

Left to right: Wild Bill, Texas Jack Omohundro, and Buffalo Bill Cody. The men were partners who put on Wild West shows. Wild Bill, however, soon tired of the business.

Wild Bill's show business career was reborn a year later. Buffalo Bill Cody asked him to act in a stage play. Wild Bill went to New York to play himself in *The Scouts of the Plains*. A dime-novel writer named Ned Buntline had dashed off the play in four hours. The script was filled with Indian raids, captive maidens, and daring rescues.

Even though he was a dreadful actor, Wild Bill was a big hit. New Yorkers hailed him as a true western hero. The pay was good, but Bill thought play-acting was silly. In one scene, the script called for him to drink some whiskey. Bill took a swig—and spit it out. The stage crew had filled the bottle with tea, not whiskey. Bill roared, "Either I get real whiskey or I ain't tellin' no story!"

The play toured eastern cities for six months. Day by day, Wild Bill's temper grew shorter. He hated the glare of the spotlight, so one night he shot it out with his pistol. On stage, he played tricks on Buffalo Bill and the other cast members. The night came at last when Bill stripped off his costume and walked out. His last words were, "I ain't going to do it anymore."

Wild Bill returned to the western plains. For a time, he and Buffalo Bill served as guides for rich English hunters. This was a restless time for Bill. He lived in the Wyoming Territory for a while. His friends knew that his vision was fading. Some said his eyes had been injured by an exploding footlight. Proud as always, Bill refused to talk about the problem.

In the spring of 1876, Wild Bill married a widow named Agnes Lake Thatcher. There had been other women in his life, but he had never settled down. Bill and Agnes, who owned a circus, had met five years earlier in Abilene. The romance had flickered off and on. Now, at last, they were man and wife.

The couple spent their honeymoon at Agnes's home in Ohio. Then Wild Bill left his bride and went off to hunt for gold. He hoped to strike it rich in the Black Hills of the Dakota Territory. A man needed money to make a home for a new wife.

As always, Wild Bill was ready to make a deal. He met with Charlie Utter and agreed to start a Black Hills freight line. While Utter worked out the details, Bill rode on to Deadwood in what is now South Dakota.

In 1876 Bill moved to the mining town of Deadwood to search for gold. Deadwood was located in the Black Hills, a region that later became part of the state of South Dakota.

The raw mining town was a rough, lawless place. Bill spent his days there searching for gold.

In Deadwood, Wild Bill crossed paths with Martha Jane Canary. Western folk knew her better as Calamity Jane. She dressed in men's clothes, smoked cigars, and ran a mining claim. Calamity had a crush on Bill and talked about him all the time. Even though he was married, she proposed that they should "join up." There is no proof that Bill returned Calamity's love. In fact, he stayed away from her as much as he could.

The outlaws and gamblers of Deadwood were worried. If Wild Bill became marshal, he would clean up the town. Bill did not want to be a lawman again, but he never backed away from a fight.

One night, six gunmen threatened to kill him. Bill whipped out his pistols and backed

Martha Jane Canary was better known as Calamity Jane. She crossed paths in Deadwood with Wild Bill. She knew Bill was married, but Calamity fell in love anyway.

the men against a wall. Calmly he told them to shut their mouths. "If you don't," he promised, "Deadwood will see some cheap funerals."

Tim Brady and Johnny Varnes were two of Wild Bill's enemies. They wanted to kill him, but they were afraid to challenge him. The safe way, they agreed, was to hire someone to do the shooting. A local tough guy named Jack McCall seemed right for the job. Brady assured McCall that he would become famous if he killed Wild Bill Hickok. To sweeten the deal the partners gave McCall a bag of gold dust.

On August 2, 1876, Wild Bill was playing poker in a Deadwood saloon. He felt nervous because he did not have his usual seat with his back to the wall. As Bill studied his cards, McCall slipped up behind him. Raising his pistol, the gunman cried, "Take that!" Then, at point-blank range, he pulled the trigger.

Wild Bill slumped to the floor. His dead fingers were holding a pair of aces and a pair of eights. Poker players who are dealt those cards still call them "the dead man's hand."

CHAPTER SEVEN

THE LEGEND OF WILD BILL HICKOK

Jack McCall did not live long enough to enjoy his newfound fame. After the shooting, he tried to hide in a butcher shop. Some say it was Calamity Jane who dragged him out to stand trial. At the trial, McCall claimed that he was avenging the death of his younger brother. The jury believed the lie and found McCall not guilty. The killer fled from Deadwood before Wild Bill's friends could catch him.

Four weeks later, McCall was arrested in Laramie, Wyoming. He had been bragging that he had killed the great Wild Bill Hickok. A judge ruled that the first trial did not count. At his new trial, the Laramie jury found McCall guilty of murder. He was hanged three months later.

The name of Wild Bill Hickok's killer soon faded, but Bill's name lives on. Unlike many western heroes Bill was well known during his lifetime. Some of the stories were more myth than fact, but his skill with a gun was real. A magazine described him as "the Prince of Pistoleers."

A bronze monument welcomes visitors to Wild Bill's gravesite in Deadwood's Mount Moriah cemetery.

Wild Bill was only thirty-nine when he died. In that short life, he was a Civil War hero, army scout, guide, lawman, and showman. He loved children and kept in close touch with his family. Would he have been a good husband and father? Death came too soon to know.

There were those who said Wild Bill was too quick on the trigger. Others said he was a crude and violent man. George Custer defended his friend. He wrote: "Whether on foot or on horseback he was one of the most perfect types of physical manhood I ever saw. . . . [M]any are the personal quarrels . . . he has checked . . . by [saying] 'This has gone far enough.'"

In 1929, the state of Illinois put up a monument at Wild Bill's birthplace. A bronze plaque says that Bill helped make the West "a safe place for women and children." The tough old lawman would have been proud of that tribute.

GLOSSARY

Border Ruffians—Raiders from Missouri who tried to turn Kansas into a slave state in the years before the Civil War.

California Gold Rush—The gold strike at Sutter's Mill in 1848 brought waves of gold-seekers to California. Only a lucky few struck it rich.

Civil War—The war fought between the North (the Union) and the South (the Confederacy), 1861–1865.

deserters—Military personnel who abandon their posts without permission.

dime novels—Low-cost magazines that printed popular fiction during the late 1800s.

dispatches—Important messages sent by military officers that were meant to be delivered quickly.

Free State Army—An armed Kansas militia set up to combat Missouri's pro-slavery Border Ruffians.

gunslingers—Outlaws and lawmen of the Wild West who settled arguments with their pistols.

jury—A group of people sworn to judge the facts and deliver a verdict in a court case.

lacrosse—An Indian game in which players catch and pass a ball using long-handled sticks with a webbed pouch at one end.

myth—A story that many people believe, but which is almost always untrue.

rebels—The soldiers and civilians who supported the South during the Civil War.

scout—A soldier who goes out ahead of an advancing army to assess the strength and location of the enemy's forces.

stampede—A sudden, headlong rush of startled animals.

town constable—A law officer who keeps the peace in a town or village.

Underground Railroad—The system of safe houses, used before the Civil War, to help runaway slaves escape to the North.

Union—The name given to the U.S. forces that fought against the South during the Civil War.

FURTHER READING

Books

Bard, Jessica. *Lawmen and Outlaws: The Wild, Wild West.* Danbury, Conn.: Children's Press, 2005.

DK Publishing. *Wild West.* New York: DK Publishing, 2005.

Fein, Eric. *High Noon: Wild Bill Hickok and the Code of the Old West.* New York: Rosen, 2003.

Rosa, Joseph G. *Wild Bill Hickok: Sharpshooter and U.S. Marshal of the Wild West.* New York: PowerKids Press, 2004.

Swanson, Wayne. *Why the West Was Wild.* Toronto: Annick Press, 2004.

Internet Addresses

Legends of America: Wild Bill Hickok and the Deadman's Hand
http://www.legendsofamerica.com/WE-BillHickok.html

Spartacus Educational: James Butler Hickok
http://www.spartacus.schoolnet.co.uk/WWhickok.htm

Wild Bill Hickok: Pistoleer, Peace Officer and Folk Hero
http://www.historynet.com/wild-bill-hickok-pistoleer-peace-officer-and-folk-hero.htm

INDEX